OLDHAM

Yorkshire Street, looking up from the very bottom at Mumps on a postcard from 1912. An open-topped tram is heading up the street towards High Street and the parish church at the top.

BRITAIN IN OLD PHOTOGRAPHS

OLDHAM

C L I F F   H A Y E S

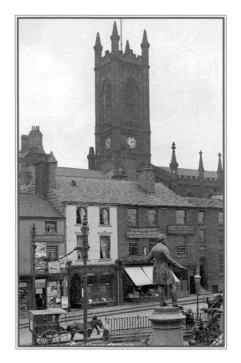

SUTTON PUBLISHING LIMITED

Sutton Publishing Limited
Phoenix Mill · Thrupp · Stroud
Gloucestershire · GL5 2BU

First published 1997

Title page photograph: High Street. St Mary's
Church dominates the scene, along with the
statue of John Platt, MP and Mayor of Oldham.

British Library Cataloguing in Publication Data
A catalogue record for this book is available from the
British Library.

ISBN 0-7509-1692-3

Typeset in 10/12 Perpetua.
Typesetting and origination by
Sutton Publishing Limited.
Printed in Great Britain by
Ebenezer Baylis, Worcester.

The very top of High Street, mid-1920s. Although the Town Hall is hidden away to the right, the Greaves
Arms shows well in the centre of the picture.

CONTENTS

The Star Inn at the bottom of George Street on King Street corner, *c.* 1890.

OLDHAM PHOTOGRAPHIC ARCHIVE

The Local Studies Photographic Archive is a collection of pictures of Oldham's past. It ranges from great historical events to everyday scenes, and documents the way life was lived in Oldham and the changes in the area over the last 150 years.

This collection of over 20,000 photographs is housed at the Local Studies Library where it is used for reference, for educational projects and, of course, for general browsing.

A copying service is available.

The Local Studies Library sells a range of publications based on the photographic collection.

Local Studies Library – Opening Hours

Monday, Thursday	10 a.m. – 7 p.m.
Tuesday	10 a.m. – 2 p.m.
Wednesday, Friday, Saturday	10 a.m. – 5 p.m.

Tel: 0161 911 4654

INTRODUCTION

Oldham was built on manufacturing, on the making of cloth in different forms. Wool, linen, cotton and cotton velvets all have their place in the town's history and all form steps in the growth of the area. Luckily these no-nonsense Northerners also became adept in the making of the machinery that was needed to do all this spinning and weaving, and led the world in the making, production and adaption of much-needed and functional engineering. The machines from Oldham could be, and still are, found all over the world and especially in the Indian sub-continent.

The strength and weakness of Oldham is the fact that it is sited on a hill, and quite a steep one at that. With today's busy life and going everywhere by car you tend to even out nature's hills and valleys, but walking around Oldham you soon come down to earth, and hilly earth at that. Catch the train to Mumps and walk up to the parish church, for example; or get off at Werneth station and walk up to Tommyfield, and you will soon feel an empathy for the travellers of old who skirted the town (causing Union Street to be created) rather than face the hill to the town centre.

Looking at the population figures, you can get a very good idea of the development of Oldham. In 1700 there were about 4,500 people living in what was the village of Oldham and the hamlets around it. Two hundred and fifty years ago in 1747 there were only 10,000 people registered living in Oldham and a lot of those were engaged in the linen manufacturing that went on in the cottage industry in which every single dwelling of the area seemed to be involved. The Parish Rolls from the time listed abodes as loom houses, bleaching houses, a woolman's house, and cloth-makers' houses, and over the years warehouses would be built next to these 'houses' so that work and home-life could be slowly separated. Oldham's first cotton mill opened as early as 1778 and the first steam engine started working in a mill over 200 years ago in 1794. It is truly amazing and puts the size of the town in context when you think that two coal pits, working and extracting coal from the bowels of the earth, could be found within 300 yards of the site of Oldham Town Hall. By 1801 the population had only risen by 2,000 in fifty years, but the next fifty years saw it at over 50,000; and by the time of the 'cotton famine' in 1863 Sir John T. Hibbert was informing the House of Commons that 'in Oldham and its outdistricts there were 111,267 of whom 39,973 were operatives. Of these only 8,028 were working full time'.

It does show the sense of character and, surprisingly to some, the deep artistic streak of Oldhamers that the artistic side and the moral side of Oldham were also very much to the fore. Oldham's first Musical Society was formed as early as 1764, and Sunday schools in Oldham were years ahead of other towns. The story of Oldham's Coliseum Theatre is a good example; it may have struggled somewhat during its existence of over a hundred years, but there were enough Oldhamers with a love of the arts and a belief that the town needed 'live' theatre to keep the thing going. Oldham had a theatre as early as 1810 when S.W. Riley opened one in Eagle Street.

As long as Oldham can keep its open-air market, and as long as Oldham people can keep that wonderful mixture of level-headedness, warmth and humour, then there is no better place in England. In the words of the '60s jingle of the battery company, 'I told 'em Oldham'.

A finely drawn sketch of the Blue Coat School, funded by Henshaw's Charity, two hundred years ago – drawn by G. Pickering and engraved by J. Tingle. The illustration is taken from *Lancashire 150 Years Ago*.

Oldham had been very much ignored by artists and photographers until the town began to grow at the end of the last century. However, we have found four drawings of Oldham from around 1870 which we feel are very worthwhile reproducing here. They give a glimpse into the Oldham that the upper class of the town wanted to portray to the outside world – a sanitised Oldham with no street beggars, no untidiness and no poor, all of which would have been around at the time.

St Mary's Church, shown here after its rebuild in 1830. This modernisation of the church was not popular with everybody. The chapels at Shaw, Royton and Crompton refused to pay the levy put on them to help finance this expensive rebuilding. Local antiquarians wrote to the local newspaper denouncing these 'upper class vandals, who took down the venerable and gothic ancient church'.

Oldham Town Hall as it appeared in 1841 when it was first constructed. It was added to and extended twice, but this shows the original Town Hall, designed in the Ionic style and said to be a replica of the Temple of Ceres in Greece. The building on the left was the local bank, and to the right is the King's Arms public house.

A sketch of Alexandra Park, just after it had opened in 1865. It was named after the Princess Alexandra of Denmark, who had recently married the very popular Prince Edward the Prince of Wales, later Edward VII. It had been built on the 'work for the Cotton Unemployed Scheme' at a cost of £31,000. The Mayor, Joseph Radcliffe, who opened the park, gave a lovely fountain for its centre, and that part became known as Mayor's Walk.

The Sun Mill off Middleton Road, on Watts Street, Chadderton, was built in 1861. Operated by Oldham Co-operators, it was enlarged by them in 1867. The architect of this, the largest mill in the district, was J. Howard. When the mill ran into trouble the £5 shares were traded as low as 4s 6d; this preceded a takeover by the Co-operative Movement. In 1915 there were 157,000 spindles on the go. Production ceased in 1959, and after catching fire in December 1985 the mill buildings were pulled down. The only reminder is the name of the Sun Mill Inn at Chadderton.

THE STREETS OF OLDHAM

The centre of Oldham is not large, but over the last hundred years, since photography became popular, most of it has changed almost out of recognition. The Spindles and Town Square shopping centres cover a lot of central Oldham, and provide a very pleasant, covered and warm shopping area, though from the outside they look a little stark and forbidding. The Old Market on Tommyfield provides a complete contrast, and the Market Hall is also a busy, bustling, friendly place.

Yorkshire Street, looking up from Mumps towards the town centre. This very early postcard was printed in Bavaria. The steepness of the street is clearly shown.

High Street and the top of Yorkshire Street, *c.* 1906. Note the sign pointing to Oldham Central station (Lancashire & Yorkshire Railways).

The bottom of Yorkshire Street, which as the caption states is called Mumps. The word comes from an old Lancashire word for a beggar, a mumper, and as this was where the first workhouse was it is probable that the word was used to denote 'where the beggars go'. Before the workhouse there was a doss-house where vagrants would be sent at sunset. The next morning they would leave at day-break, and as soon as they got through the doors they would start begging, or 'mumping'.

Looking down Yorkshire Street. This view is from a war-time card printed in 1940, complete with a stirring message on the reverse from the Prime Minister. I suspect the photograph is from about 1939 because of the number of excursions advertised outside the Holt Yelloway offices next to the square, white Oldham Hotel on the very left of the picture.

High Street, c. 1905. Even though the tram lines have been laid, the town still presents a quiet picture.

The top of High Street, from a 1950s postcard; again, though, I suspect that the photograph is earlier. F. W. Woolworth's is prominent on the left next to Timothy Whites & Taylor's shop. Woolworth's opened here in 1925 and was enlarged to the size seen here soon after. In October 1983 the Council granted permission for the building to be pulled down, and after the January sales in 1984 Woolies finally closed.

The very top of High Street, which once ran on to Manchester Road. George Street was to the right and the strangely named Priests' Hill to the left. These were the days when you parked outside the shop that you were going to, if you were lucky enough to have a car.

'Mumps Oldham' says the title on the card, and Mumps and Oldham it is. Do not let the railway station drag you away towards Rhodes Bank; Mumps is the bottom of Yorkshire Street and the bottom of Rock Street, though it is now cut in half by St Mary's Way. Yorkshire Street used to continue down to Huddersfield Road and Lees Road, but now the bottom bit carries the name of the area – Mumps.

The main road in and out of Oldham has changed over the years; there is just a little bit of the original left. It runs down between the Greaves Arms and St Mary's Church, and is called Church Road. Walking down this road you can imagine when this was the highway to Yorkshire and the east.

This picture is from about 1930. The Holt Yelloway offices are offering trips to Blackpool, and the Dean & Dawson's shop across the road is attracting attention to its window display.

High Street, very late 1950s. The Co-operative Self Service has arrived next to Boot's Chemist on the right of the picture. Peter Street is just to the right. Most of that street vanished along with St Peter's Church during redevelopment of central Oldham. The St Peter Street redevelopment was labelled CDA-1 and re-opened as the St Peter's Shopping Scheme in 1968. It was not a success, and has now gone. The Dr Syntax public house at the top of Peter Street is one of the bits that remain. The Dr Syntax was named after a villain in a Victorian novel.

Rhodes Bank, looking down Mumps to the railway bridge at the bottom and Huddersfield Road beyond, c. 1896. This area between Mumps and Rhodes Bank was a very popular shopping area, with Buckley & Proctor's Mumps Bazaar, and a variety of other little specialist shops. Of course the more select shopping was done along High Street in the town centre.

Market Place was the top of High Street and this is the view from 1903, though I suggest that some of the figures in the foreground were painted on afterwards, a common practice in early photography. George Street drops away to the left and the tram is waiting to take that route, probably to Grains Bar. Manchester Road is straight ahead. The ornamental sign sticking out from behind the tram is on the drinking fountain that can now be found inside Alexandra Park.

Another view of the Market Place, c. 1905. You can see clearly now Hulme's Cash Chemist and the fancy drinking fountain that graced the top of Manchester Road. The Old Cheshire Cheese Inn can be seen to the right of the open-topped tram, which is waiting to leave for Manchester. Hulme's Chemist later became Stevens' Chemist, and the buildings were cleared away in the summer of 1931.

Market Place, *c.* 1906. This time the photographer was standing in Manchester Road outside the Cheshire Cheese, looking back into the Square. Hulme's Chemist is on the right and the Lancashire Clog Company next door. The Red Lion can be seen on the left of our picture, on the corner of Henshaw Street.

Market Place, just before the Second World War. This is from almost the same spot as the photograph above, but nearly half a century later. The Red Lion has now gone, replaced by Burton's building, with Meesons' sweetshop tucked in on the corner.

Market Place, from the top of the hill looking down Manchester Street, early 1960s. The Regent Hotel (Gartside Ales) now stands on the site of Hulme's (see page 17), and the Prince William Hotel is on the very right where the Cheshire Cheese once stood.

Market Place, 1960s. Although to many of us this is a modern picture, it was taken over thirty years ago. For a time this area was referred to as Old Market Place, when attempts were made to move all activities to the Church Terrace area outside the Town Hall, and to call that New Market Place. This was not a popular move.

King Street, *c.* 1930. The photographer was looking away from Manchester Street towards the junction with Union Street at the bottom. That is Barn Street coming in on the left, and the buildings on the right are the Bingo and Co-operative complex.

King Street, from the junction with Union Street, with King Street Baptist Chapel on the left, 1905. That is not a horse tram coming down King Street; on close inspection you will see that it is a horse-drawn cart trotting along in front of one of the new electric trams. The wires and tram lines of Union Street can be made out crossing the picture.

Union Street, the Rhodes Bank end, showing the Palace Theatre in 1909 just after it had opened in November 1908. All the big names of the day appeared at the Palace – George Formby snr and jnr, and Gracie Fields, to name just three. It later became the Odeon Cinema, which closed down in October 1983 and was demolished in 1992. Union Street was opened as a bypass when the town centre became busy over a century ago. It was popular with through horse traffic because it cut out the climb up to Market Place.

The middle part of Union Street, 1906 or 1907. The Prudential Assurance building, designed and built in 1901 by Alfred Waterhouse of Manchester and Rochdale town halls fame, is on the left of the picture. Luckily it is still standing today. As you look north you can see the ornamental spire of Queen Street Congregational Church in the distance.

Union Street looking north, 1919. The Methodist Chapel, built in about 1875, is on the very right of the picture. This is now the Brunswick Square development (built in 1985), which retains the archway and fountain from the old chapel in a lovely little courtyard. The Grosvenor Cinema can be seen under construction in the centre left of the photograph. This opened in August 1920 and closed down as a cinema in August 1961. It was later the Cat's Whiskers Night Club, then Eddie's Place, and finally closed as Bo Bo's Night Spot, being demolished in July 1985. Oldham Job Centre is now on the site.

Union Street, probably a century ago. That's the Young Men's Christian Association above A. Goss's tailor's shop, with the Royal Oak inn next door but one.

Union Street, very early 1960s. The foundation stone for the Lyceum building on the right, designed by N.G. Pennington, was laid in 1855 by James Platt, and the building was opened a year later. The Lyceum today is the original building together with the extension that was grafted on in 1881, given by the grandsons of James Platt. The Oldham MBC now own and look after this building, which has been cleaned since this picture was taken. Note the square bus shelters outside the Lyceum. Clegg Street corner shows well, as do the towers on the Prudential Building. The designer of this, Alfred Waterhouse, loved very red brick and would stipulate 'blood red brick' on his plans; this led to the nickname 'Slaughterhouse Waterhouse' among his fellow architects. You can also make out the white cupola that graced the Grosvenor Cinema beyond, which was probably already closed by the time this picture was taken. The dome was taken down before the venue re-opened as the Cat's Whiskers Night Club.

This is the street that was popular with the youth of the town, who would don their best clothes and go 'promenading' at weekends. It later became called the 'Monkey Run', when best suits were nicknamed monkey suits; many an Oldham marriage started with shy glances and awkward introductions on Union Street.

The Oldham Lyceum before the second part was grafted on, but showing the first extension to it, a School of Science & Art, which opened in 1865. This picture is probably from the 1870s. The building also had a basement gymnasium: the Lyceum has always led the way with its facilities for members, as the page of a Prospectus from 1913 (below) shows.

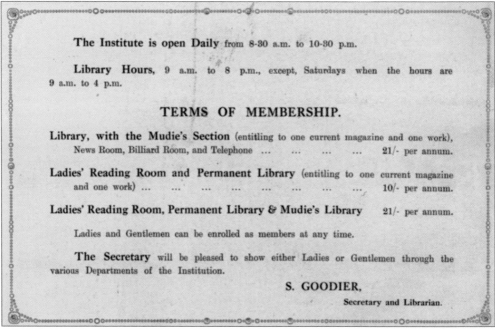

The Institute is open Daily from 8-30 a.m. to 10-30 p.m.

Library Hours, 9 a.m. to 8 p.m., except, Saturdays when the hours are 9 a.m. to 4 p.m.

TERMS OF MEMBERSHIP.

Library, with the Mudie's Section (entitling to one current magazine and one work), News Room, Billiard Room, and Telephone ... ... 21/- per annum.

Ladies' Reading Room and Permanent Library (entitling to one current magazine and one work) ... ... 10/- per annum.

Ladies' Reading Room, Permanent Library & Mudie's Library 21/- per annum.

Ladies and Gentlemen can be enrolled as members at any time.

The Secretary will be pleased to show either Ladies or Gentlemen through the various Departments of the Institution.

S. GOODIER,

Secretary and Librarian.

From 8.30 a.m. until 10.30 p.m. was a long day, but a great service for the members. I wonder what happened if you wanted two current magazines at one time.

Another of the amenities to tempt you into joining the Lyceum in 1913: the library.

The view of the Lyceum used for the cover of the Prospectus, 1913.

The Star Inn, *c.* 1920. The photographer stood on King Street to take this picture. You have George Street, formerly Bardsley Brow, to the right of the hotel, and King Street to the left. The no. 7 tram can be seen returning from Summit, and you can just make out the veranda of the Grand Theatre on the right.

The very bottom of King Street, early 1920s. The Paragon garage on the left was a well-known landmark until it was cleared away in the mid-1980s. You can see the Star Inn in the background and of course to the right is the Grand Theatre, destined in 1937 to be the Gaumont Cinema; later it had many other names and uses, including a ten pin bowling alley and a nightclub.

A very early postcard looking up Curzon Street from High Street corner. The building across the top is the original Market Hall, built in 1856 by a private company. As the company showed no profit, it sold the hall to the Corporation in 1865 for £10,654 10s. The Market Hall seen on this picture was closed in September 1904 to be replaced by a more solid building.

Curzon Street, looking towards the new Market Hall, c. 1909. The new hall was opened on 6 April 1906 by Councillor Henshaw, who unlocked the Henshaw Street doors with a 'golden key', and declared it open. This card was published for Hyde & Son who had a stall inside the Market Hall, and printed at 'Our Works in Saxony' – a practice that was soon to finish with the onset of the First World War.

A very busy Curzon Street, on this Edwardian postcard. It shows the new Market Hall at the top on Albion Street, with the Albion Hotel on the right. The street in this photograph is full of people who seem to be socialising rather than shopping.

Albion Street, with the Market Hall on the right, June 1970. The picture was taken from Curzon Street corner with Henshaw Street running across the top. This picture shows the detail of the work on the Market Hall front, which unfortunately went up in flames on the evening of Saturday 5 October 1974. It was a bitter blow to Oldham and its shoppers.

High Street, from the Town Hall steps, *c.* 1875. The statue is that of John Platt, Mayor, MP, benefactor and owner of Platt Brothers, the leading engineering firm in the town. This statue was put up with great pride by the citizens of Oldham. Today it can be found in Alexandra Park.

High Street, late 1880s. Horse-drawn buses have become a regular feature, laboriously plying up and down Oldham's steep streets. The imposing statue of John Platt can be seen on the right of the picture, looking down the High Street towards Mumps, past the fine Ionic-fronted Town Hall.

High Street, *c.* 1935. There was a great variety of shops along the street, all of which were swept away not long after this picture was taken.

The top of Yorkshire Street from Waterloo Road, 1890. The fact that the parish church dominates the highest point of the town is well illustrated in this photograph.

High Street, outside the Town Hall, *c.* 1905. The main post office was actually in the Town Hall at this time, and the large telegraph pole on top of the building can be seen quite clearly. The statue of John Platt stands in front of the Kings Arms Hotel, surrounded by railings and potted plants.

Church Terrace, *c.* 1930. In front of the parish church is the War Memorial, with the front of the rebuilt Greaves Hotel on the right.

Yorkshire Street, *c.* 1905. Again the figures in the foreground were painted on to give the picture more life, but the open-topped electric Corporation tram is real enough.

The Union Street (left) and Yorkshire Street (right) junction, with Bow Street in the middle, *c.* 1912. The three young lads, who were obviously watching the photographer, were probably scattered as that horse-drawn cart lumbered up behind them.

Queen's Road, alongside and almost inside Alexandra Park. These houses were built for the upper middle class of Oldham and enjoyed their position within the park gates. The road is a little cut off today, being the far side of Oldham Way.

Huddersfield Road, 1920s. This is the other side of Mumps Bridge, away from the town centre. The road coming in on the left, with a policeman on traffic duty, is the road to Lees and Greenfield.

The climb up Yorkshire Street into High Street is clearly shown here, on this Edwardian postcard from around 1904. The Town Hall steps with their lovely gas lamps can be seen on the right of the picture; to the left you can see how the street level was cut 10 ft lower than the level outside the Greaves Arms in an effort to ease the gradient. The ornamental cable post for the electric trams shows up well against the sky in this picture, and is typical of the civic pride that Oldham people had.

As well as the donkey cart in the middle of the picture the horse-drawn hackney carriages can be seen behind, waiting for their next fare. The small building on the right of the cabs is the drivers' shelter.

CIVIC PRIDE

There was a bit of a tussle before the granting of a Charter of Incorporation to Oldham in 1849. The Select Vestry thought that they knew best, and things should be left under their jurisdiction. They maintained that Oldham did not need Incorporation as they could adequately look after the area themselves. As we come up to the 150th anniversary of the granting of that Charter, in 1999, one thing we can say for definite is that both sides in the argument for and against Incorporation had great pride both in the area and in the new burgeoning town of Oldham. It is clear as you look back over Oldham's history how strong the feelings of civic pride were.

Oldham's Charter, 1849.

Oldham Town Hall and the War Memorial, 1960s. Oldham was one of the few places that actually had a Town Hall eight years before it became a town. The battle for Incorporation was a strong one and well worth pursuing. Even though the Chartists won and the town received its Charter of Incorporation in 1849, the Chartists were defeated by the anti-incorporators in the first municipal elections.

The War Memorial, standing between the parish church and the Town Hall, is in a most prominent, and therefore ideal, position. The memorial is considered by many to be one of the finest in northern England. (See also pages 70 and 71.)

The Art Gallery, 1910. This building was put up in 1883 to a design by Thomas Mitchell, a local architect. It was opened by Sir John Lubbock (later Lord Avebury), who was to go down in history as the man who introduced bank holidays.

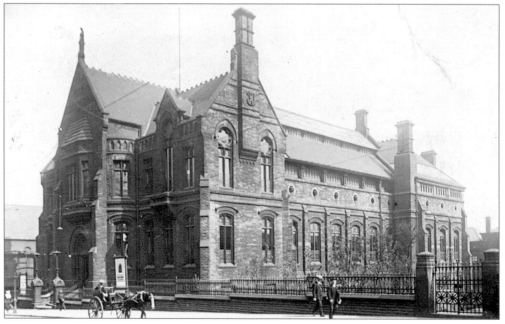

This is the same building as above, but the caption on the card says it is the 'Free Library' – which of course it was; it was both Art Gallery and Free Library. It cost £26,748 to build originally and an extra £8,840 for the extension in 1894. The dots along the side are reliefs of famous men in the literary and art world. Look for the head of William Shakespeare, who we are told in his lifetime spelt his name 26 different ways including, I expect, the way it is here, not our usually accepted way.

The Post Office, Union Street. Built earlier than the Art Gallery next door, it was started in 1875 when the amenities in the post office in Greaves Street proved too cramped, and opened in 1877. Today it is well known as the Local History Library, one of the best and most helpful in Lancashire.

The Public Baths, Union Street, were built in 1854 and extended in 1880, with a lovely French pavilion roof. They were built as a monument to Sir Robert Peel, and were a much more functional memorial than a statue. In the foyer is a marble bust of Sir Robert, by Alexandra Munro, with an inscription on the plinth underneath it. The cost of the building was met by public subscription of £1,066, and a further £4,000 given by the Corporation; £900 of that was given by the Peel Committee itself. By the 1920s these baths contained a Remedial Department with Turkish baths, foam baths, sulphur foam baths, iodine aeration baths, radiant heat and infra-red electric treatment, all supervised by fully qualified staff and a great benefit to people suffering from arthritis and rheumatism.

The Lyceum building, across the road from the Baths on the previous picture, and one of the few buildings on Union Street to survive. The Baths, Post Office and Art Gallery are all on the right of the picture, and the fancy spire in the distance is the Queen Street Congregational Chapel. Note the decorative touches of the ornamental lamps on pedestals outside the Lyceum building.

The Grammar School, on a 1918 postcard. The foundation stone of this building was laid in September 1893, and Earl Spencer opened the building in May 1895. The origins of the Grammar School go back to 1606, and to a building alongside today's market, on the site of Peter Street.

The Infirmary, *c.* 1900. The original building was on Union Street West, and was started with a grant of £1,000 from the left-overs of a fund for starving Lancashire workers who would rather have no cotton than cotton picked by badly treated slaves during the American Civil War. The building itself was started in 1870; it opened in 1873 and was further extended in 1877. It received the Royal prefix earlier this century.

Boundary Park Hospital, Rochdale Road, 1930. This building started out as a workhouse infirmary. In April 1930 the Board of Guardians handed it over to the Health Committee and it went from strength to strength especially during the Second World War. On 5 July 1945 it passed into the hands of the new National Health Service.

Blue Coat School, Oldham, mid-1930s. This very large building was on Oldham Edge, and a very fine building it was with its battlements, rounded towers and gate-house. In 1807 Thomas Henshaw, a wealthy hatter, left a bequest of £40,000, at the time an enormous amount, to build a Grammar School, but only if the people of Oldham gave the site. The heirs of Thomas Henshaw, who were expecting to be left large amounts of money on his death, disputed the will and its £40,000 bequest. The argument dragged on until 1830, when work on the building was at last able to begin. During this time the money had grown to an amazing £100,000. In its first year 102 poor boys between the ages of nine and eleven were admitted to the school.

The Henshaw Blue Coat School, Edgerton Street, early 1930s. This unusual photograph shows the boys from the Boarding School lined up on the fire escapes and on the street behind the imposing building.

Robin Hill Wash-house on Dunbar Street, 1948. The Council were proud of the amenities they provided, and there were wash-houses like this at Mortar Street, Waterhead, and Heron Street, Hollinwood. The area desperately needed a wash-house when Robin Hill opened in 1905. Waterhead followed in 1925 and Hollinwood in April 1932.

'Smoky Oldham', 1920. Not much civic pride in this photograph you may think, but Oldham was proud of just how hard-working it was: '220 Chimneys in Oldham and all smoking' was a proud boast. They used to joke that the only time you got a clear view of Oldham was during Wakes Week.

OLDHAM WAKES & MARKET

In ancient times patron saints of churches would be celebrated on their day by a night of fasting and prayer. To encourage people to join in, a day of games and pleasure and a day off work afterwards were promised. For staying awake all night they would have a 'wake' festival. The day became two days, and then a week and so Wakes Weeks came into being. Most Lancashire Wakes Weeks take place on or around the day of the saint to which the local parish church is dedicated. The original dedication for Oldham's church was the Blessed Mary of Assumption, and her day is 15 August. From 1800 to 1946 Oldham celebrated its Wakes Week during the last week of August, the difference being explained by the eleven days that England 'lost' when the new calendar was introduced in 1752.

Oldham Wakes, 1905. It was a stay-at-home holiday for most people, with only the upper and management classes going to the seaside.

Another very early postcard of Oldham Wakes, 1900.

The Rushcart at High Crompton, Shaw, August 1907. Rushbearing was an ancient custom to clean and refresh the church, and was tied into the patron's day. For Oldham it was 15 August, being St Mary's Day or the Feast of the Assumption. Until 1801 the church had a plain clay floor, and rushes were spread to keep in the warm and to soak up the wet, so that the clay did not turn to mud. In 1801 the authorities in Oldham cancelled this festival as they had laid flagstones in the church, thrown out the old rushes and did not want fresh ones. This was not a popular decision: riots ensued and six people were killed. By 1829 the tradition had returned, and continued on and off until 1876. Even today it is brought back from time to time.

TOMMY FIELDS MARKET, OLDHAM.

Tommyfield (which has become two words on the card) Open Market, *c.* 1900. Oldham was not thought to be large enough or important enough to be granted a charter for a market, but business had to go on. Traders would set up in High Street Square, and visiting butchers and fishmongers would tout their wares there, alongside the farmers who brought in their produce. In the middle of the last century, in about 1856, Oldham's first Market Hall was built by a private consortium, but it was soon sold to the newly formed Corporation in 1865. Market days were traditionally Monday, Friday and Saturday, and two large fairs were also held on the Green in June and September.

The piece of land behind the Albion Inn, called Curzon Field, was chosen as the site for a market when in 1833 the town's Select Vestry became demanding and tried to impose unreasonable regulations, which irritated the traders in the Old and New Market Squares. The field was nicknamed 'Owd Tommy's Field' after Thomas Whittaker, who rented the field from the Curzon family to keep pigs. The land was part of the Roundthorn Estate, which the Curzon family had acquired in 1716 when Sir Nathaniel Curzon married Mary Assheton.

This postcard from about 1904 shows the outside market, or the 'Outside Stall Ground'.

Tommyfield Market, 1910. The market had a good reputation for its fresh produce, and as the shoppers wandered round the varied stalls they would probably have a snack of new potatoes with mint sauce and pease pudding, or steaming hot black pudding freshly imported from nearby Bury.

A bustling picture of Albion Street, *c.* 1910. Tommyfield Open Market is on the right of the picture. The large Market Hall behind was Oldham's second (see pages 27 and 28).

Tommyfield Market, 1960s: nothing swinging about the market here, and plenty of headscarves in view. The market at Tommyfield is still thriving and very busy today. It is open on an extra day as a flea market.

A festival at Delph, July 1911. You can make out the word Zeplin on a poster on the front of the cart. The writer of this card was Florrie, and she was writing to her sister Annie Bilcliffe, who was in the Mosley Ward of the Royal Infirmary. She told her that all the family were in this picture, and that she had marked 'father' with a cross: that must be him with the big moustache, looking at the camera.

The Whit Walks at Glodwick, 1950s. The Rose Queen proudly heads the procession with the local brass band behind. These processions at Whitsuntide were a popular feature in the northern towns, and date back to the early nineteenth century. Some parishes in the area still hold Whit Walks.

THE CHURCHES

Oldham is a part of the archdeaconry and bishopric of Manchester and a parochial chapelry in the parish of Prestwich-cum-Oldham. Mention of a church or chapel on this site goes back to 1280 when a transfer of land, to include 'the chapel at Oldham', was witnessed by Oldham's first vicar, William Scherewind. In 1476 the church was rebuilt, paid for by Ralph Langley, 'Parson of the Kyrke of Prestwich'. By the early nineteenth century, when Oldham was fast becoming a booming industrial town, some of its leading citizens decided that they deserved a much grander church than the tatty old one they had. Their plans for a new church met with strong opposition, until 3 July 1825: there was panic at the church when a stone from the tower fell through the roof during a service, and one of the congregation noticed cracks in the walls, with daylight showing through them. The congregation stood their ground for a while and then panicked and fled the church. Some reports say they broke windows and fought to get out, but the whole incident could have been engineered to push the re-building through. On 29 July 1827 the last sermon was preached, and the new, re-built St Mary's opened in 1830. Some historians maintain that the tower was left almost untouched, as its architecture seems much older than the rest of the church.

St Mary's Church, 1912. The present structure, started in 1827, was erected at a cost of £30,000. The small, square building to the left was the Greaves Arms.

This card is from 1922 and was issued jointly by St Mary's Church and the bellfounders, John Taylor & Company, to commemorate the re-casting of the bells. This is the tenor, largest of the twelve re-cast bells and, at 35 cwt 4 lb, the heaviest. The inscription on the bell reads: 'Frederick Houghton JP Mayor, 1922; William Temple, Bishop of Manchester; Ambrose J. Wilson, Vicar; John Booth, Albert Cheetham, William Perkins JP, Albert Haigh (Wardens); James Mallalieu, Samuel Elson (Sidesmen).'

Over the past few years I have visited this fascinating church many times, and have always had a very warm welcome. Twice a year they have an open day, when the general public have an opportunity to see the crypt with its fourteenth-century knight's stone coffin, and also pay their respects to the 'Oldham Giant'. This view is of one of the two main corridors down there.

St Thomas' Church, Moorside, was built in 1872 and paid for completely by Thomas Mellowdew, with his brother James donating the bells and the clock. Before this church was built the people from the 'small, bleak and unlovely mining village' had to worship in the village school.

St James' Church, Greenacres, 1905. Designed by Goodwin, the church incorporated pre-made cast-iron parts. The foundation stone was laid on 3 September 1827 by James Lee of Higher Clerksfield, and the church, which could seat 1,500, was opened and dedicated on 19 September 1829 by the Bishop of Chester, Dr Sumner. It became a separate parish in 1835.

St Peter's Church, Peter Street, 1912. This church was originally built by public subscription as a chapel-of-ease for the parish church. It is unusual for a chapel-of-ease to be built so near to the parish church, but far be it from me to suggest that it was built to encourage the poor of the parish to worship there, leaving the upper classes to St Mary's. St Peter's opened on 2 June 1768 and was enlarged in 1804. It was again enlarged, with what was for Oldham unusual splendour, at a cost of £16,400 in 1899 and re-opened in 1901. It was known for some years as 'Winter's Church', from the Revd William Winter, vicar there for forty-two years from the start of the nineteenth century.

This postcard shows the rebuilt church as it was until it closed in 1963. There was a plan to take the whole church, stone by stone, out to Limeside for the new housing estate there. Everyone thought it a wonderful idea to save this 'most beautiful of Oldham's churches', but when it came to paying for it, no one stepped forward to offer the £80,000 needed. In the end the 'Great Bell of St Peter' was hung in St Chad's at Limeside, and new homes were found for nearly all of the church's furniture – except for the font, which proved too large and heavy to move and was broken up on the spot. Some of the stained glass windows ended up in Meaford, Ontario, Canada, in the chapel at Lakeview Cemetery. One memory of St Peter's is from 25 March 1842, when it was recorded that 840 baptisms had taken place on that day, the one day in the year that this church did not charge. I believe that the kindly Mr Winter thought that the saving of 1s for 'churching' would be a great relief to the poor people in his parish, and had actually held some services over the weeks before, not entering them in the records until the 'free day'.

An unusual postcard showing the inside of St Mary's Catholic Church, opened on Shaw Road in 1838. In 1829, when the Freedom of Worship Act was passed in England, a small Catholic chapel had opened in Lord Street.

The Wesleyan Chapel and School, at Shaw, c. 1900. Around the middle of the eighteenth century Methodism arrived in Oldham, but the first ministers were not welcomed and were abused, pushed about and even arrested. The first Wesleyan Methodist Chapel was built in 1775, and on Sunday 4 April 1779 (Easter Day) John Wesley himself came to Oldham and was well received. He wrote favourably of the town in his diary. He came again on Friday 2 April 1790 to open the chapel in Manchester Street.

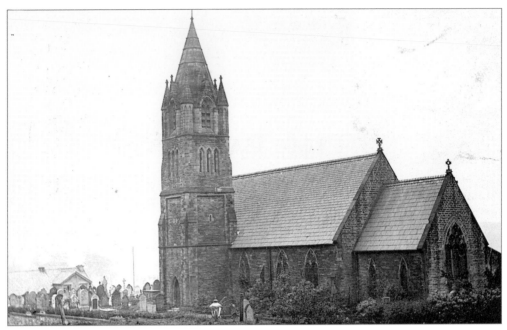

Christ Church, Chadderton, 1905.

THE OLD CHURCH STANDS AS IN DAYS OF OLD,
WHERE WORTHY CITIZENS MEET
WITH GRATEFUL HEARTS, TO OFFER THANKS
THE HAPPY FUTURE GREET.

OLDHAM CHURCH AND YORKSHIRE STREET IN 1760.

Oldham in 1760, showing the commanding position of the church looking down over the community. Many books state that the church was originally dedicated to All Saints, but this would have meant that Oldham Wakes were at the end of November, which would not have been popular. There are hundreds of stories to tell about the place – for example, the choir going on strike, the vicar being thrown out for not signing a contract, the mayor who refused to go to church, the sexton who could not dig graves in February 1683 because the ground was so frozen, and put six bodies to rest under stones in the porch, and of course 'Big Dody', a lovely man and a gentle person – 37 stone and buried three times (not to be confused with the Oldham Giant). The view from the top of the tower is magnificent: vicars in the past could spot sinners almost as far as Middleton. Don't forget, churches are open on Sundays as well, and many are open on Sunday afternoons for visitors.

SECTION FIVE

THE PARKS

When you have a village which is surrounded by countryside and you have a central area for meetings and gatherings, then the need for a public park does not exist. When an area becomes industrialised, and tightly packed houses and factories appear, then there is a need for even the poorest to have a chance to smell the roses and flowers. Parks became a welcome amenity for this very reason.
When you think of parks in Oldham, you automatically think of Alexandra Park, but there was a recreation ground before that, on an open area off Union Street, near the Art Gallery.

The glory and beauty of Alexandra Park, Oldham, 1930s.

The entrance to Alexandra Park, 1905. The large area outside the gates was planned so that horse-drawn omnibuses and private carriages could pull up and let their passengers alight to enter the delights of 'the largest and most elaborate of the great Northern Civic Monuments'. It soon became known as Speaker's Corner, and on Saturday and Sunday afternoons and even summer evenings the crowds would gather to listen to the latest political arguments or the airings of unrest. Ramsay MacDonald and Winston Churchill are just two of the great orators of the day who held the crowd on this spot.

The Government announced in 1862 that a 3½ per cent interest loan was available for schemes of 'Public Interest which would keep unemployed men busy'. Oldham applied and received money, and then set about reviving a plan for a public park which had foundered some fifteen years earlier because of lack of money. The Council approached the Revd John Cocker, who owned the Swine Clough Estate (57 acres), which had been in the Ogden family for over 300 years. They offered £10,750, which he accepted. A further 15 acres was added and work began. They started first by culverting Sheep Wash Brook and then laying out the park to a design by local architects Woodhouse & Potts.

Oldham was very proud of Alexandra Park, and rightly so. Postcards like this one from the 1930s, which showed the lovely gardens which bloomed in the middle of all the smoke and grime in Oldham, were very popular, and sent with a chuckle by many a visitor to the town. Work on the park started in 1863 with the first sod being cut by the Mayor, John Riley. The total cost amounted to around £31,000.

A slightly earlier card but with the same surprise 'this is Oldham' message on the back. Alexandra Park opened on a miserable wet Monday, 28 August 1865. Officials and local dignitaries gathered at the Town Hall, and in spite of the heavy rain led a procession to the park where they placed a time capsule of coins of the day and other memorabilia under the foundation stone of the Lodge. Then they processed around the park itself.

The refreshment rooms, Alexandra Park, pre-First World War. The rooms were at the far end of the Top Walk and were designed after the continental style of pavement café; they were noted for their afternoon teas. The Top Walk was known as 'one of the finest in the whole of Lancashire'.

Almost the same view as the picture above, but 1941. With its statues, views and of course the famous 'lions' den', the Top Walk was always a popular place to do a spot of courting. If a young man asked you to walk with him on Top Walk and then invited you to sit for a while in the 'den', then he was serious. If those statues of lions could only talk!

The Ashcroft monument, on Top Walk, Alexandra Park, 1911. Unveiled in 1903, it was designed by E.W. Pomeroy and paid for by the 'people' of Oldham. The inscription on the plinth shows how high this Oldham MP was held in their esteem. It simply says: 'Robert Ashcroft, MP for Oldham 1895–1899, "The Workers' Friend".' (See also page 77.)

The statue of Joseph Howarth, 'Blind Joe', Oldham's Bellman for over forty years. Joe died on 17 May 1862 and this statue was unveiled on 9 May 1868. He was a Methodist lay preacher, very honest and straightforward, and a bit dour. His party piece was reciting whole chapters of the Bible verbatim. He would not be amused by the local folk legend which says that his statue has a 10s (ten bob) note under the right foot, and that it lifts up at midnight on a full moon! Well, that was the story a century ago.

The boating lake, Alexandra Park, *c.* 1939. When the park was opened in 1865 the lake area was Snipe Clough Refuse Tip. It was converted into a boating lake at a cost of £14,000 and opened in 1903.

The boating lake in Alexandra Park, 1960s. The lake covers 4.5 acres, and the upkeep of the boat house and the number and variety of boats for hire has differed wildly over this century. It would surely make a great millennium project to restore the boat house and its facilities.

The ornamental bridge in Werneth Park. This park was given to the Corporation by Miss Marjory Lees and was opened to the public on 30 May 1936 by the Mayor, Alderman J.R. Bainbridge. It was a very formal park, with terraces and shrubberies all beautifully laid out. It had a conservatory and music room that was used by many local societies.

Crime Lake, down at Woodhouse Green, 1930s. The lake was dug specifically to keep the Fairbottom Branch Canal topped up, but became a very popular place for days out.

One of the furthest parks from Oldham is Dun Wood Park up at Crompton: this is the entrance, shown on a postcard from 1915. The lovely named area 'Goats' is up there along with Wood End, Crompton Fold and Jubilee. One well-behaved citizen is obeying the notice board which forbids bicycles, and has left his outside.

The flower beds and children's playground in Dun Wood Park, 1910. It also shows the wildness of the area around the park, with Whitefield Farm and Top of the Hill behind.

Two more views of Dun Wood Park. The plaque next to the gates declares that the park was presented to Crompton Urban District Council by Capt. Abram Crompton JP, on behalf of himself and his relatives, the Crompton-Cheethams, on the Coronation of George V, 22 June 1911. It was opened on 14 September 1912. Can you make out the railway signals on the line to Newhey and Rochdale, which runs alongside the park? Below is another card of the park from the same set.

Just for the record there were other parks in the area, including Copster Park (16¾ acres), opened 17 June 1911; Westwood Park (formerly Hudson Fold), opened 26 March 1924 and on the site of the playing fields where Oldham County FC and Pine Villa FC (who later became Oldham Athletic FC) played their games around a century ago; Waterhead Park, opened 17 July 1926; Limeside Park (17¾ acres), opened 18 August 1932; Bishop Park (50 acres) at Grains Bar, given by Mr and Mrs Ludlam of Ashton in memory of Mrs Ludlam's parents, Mr and Mrs Bishop; and lastly there is Werneth Park, given by Miss Marjory Lees.

Daisy Nook, though only just in Oldham, was definitely thought of as *the* place for Oldhamers to spend the day on a summer weekend or bank holiday. Above is a 1905 postcard showing a very rural Daisy Nook, but showing a sign for 'Pots of Tea', etc. Below is a postcard from 1909 showing more of the charms of Daisy Nook with the River Medlock in the fore. Today Daisy Nook is a National Trust country park, and there is a very good garden centre where the swing-boats and helter-skelter were.

Waterhouses was the original name of the hamlet which Ben Brierley's story 'A Day Out', turned into Daisy Nook. Above is a 1910 view of the area.

Foxdenton Hall Park, Chadderton, showing the bowling green in front of the hall, 1963. Foxdenton Hall off Foxdenton Lane was built in about 1620, and though much altered and added to forms the basis of today's hall. Home of the Radcliffes of Urmston, it was leased to Chadderton Council by the family in 1922 and opened to the public.

The lake, Foxdenton Park, 1930s. The lake is not large but adds charm to the park. The Council only rented the estate, and by the time they had purchased the park in 1960 the hall itself was in a very poor state; in fact it was dangerous and liable to fall down. There was a vigorous debate about whether the hall was worth saving, and luckily money was found for its restoration. By 1965 the hall was in tip-top condition again.

The putting green, Foxdenton Park, 1920s. The green was soon replaced by a tennis court. The Radcliffe family were noted for their strong and fearless qualities. Alexandra Radcliffe (1677–1735), who built the present (second) hall, was one, as was the 'Foxdenton Redhead', Col. Sir William Radcliffe, a loyal supporter of Charles I.

Royton Hall, 1914. The hall was owned by the Byron family until 1662, and at that time it was a real mish-mash of brick, stone and wood. It was demolished in 1939.

PEOPLE & EVENTS

History books tell us how quickly Oldham rose from being a small village on a hill to a mighty industrial town. History also tells of Oldham's industry and its diversification into engineering. What history does not convey is the 'spirit' of the people of Oldham: the warmth and friendliness, but always a willingness for a good debate. The people accepted that clearing away old industrial practices and starting again was necessary for their survival, and there cannot be many towns that have had the spirit to do that, as Oldham has. Where you have this energy there will always be plenty of events and characters to record.

An event held at the Watersheddings (Oldham's rugby ground) when youngsters demonstrated the grand old art of maypole dancing, July 1911. I don't have a clue what the occasion was, but on the back of the card is written 'Lilian Bates', which could have been a dancing school or the name of one of the girls taking part.

In the summer of 1913 King George V and Queen Mary arranged to stay with Lord Derby at Knowsley Hall for a week so they could visit the industrial towns of Lancashire. Oldham, Bury, Ashton and Wigan were all visited and each town competed with the others to make sure that their visit would be the most memorable one. Here we see the royal cortège entering Oldham on 12 July 1913. Little did they know that the Lancashire Fusiliers drawn up so proudly to welcome the royal party would be wanted at the front to fight within twelve months of this picture.

The King and Queen were welcomed to the works of Platt Brothers, where they met the owners and toured the factory. Lord Derby can be seen in this picture next to the factory girl in the clean white pinny on the far right. I'll bet she bought quite a few of these postcards, which were produced by Allen & Sons of Oldham.

Oldham turned out in style for the first royal visit by a reigning monarch. A grand podium was put up outside the Town Hall, and the elite of Oldham's society gathered round to see their King and Queen. Joseph Ashworth was Mayor of Oldham at the time, and can be seen here. In the top right-hand corner of the picture you can see men sitting on the roof-top for a better view.

Crowds lined every inch of the royal route when Oldham received its King and Queen. Factories closed or gave time off; schools turned out en masse. It was a proud day, and a day, no doubt, never to be repeated.

Oldham unveiled its memorial to the 'Pals' who had made the supreme sacrifice and given their lives in the First World War on 28 April 1923. There was not a dry eye in Oldham, as soldiers, sailors, airmen and cadets turned out to show their respect. Here we see the scene in a very crowded Yorkshire Street, looking down from the Town Hall.

The dedication of the War Memorial. The bronze statue by Albert Toft with its fine granite base, standing in its unique setting, was unveiled by Gen. Ian Hamilton, and dedicated to the three battalions of the Manchester Regiment raised in Oldham (the 1st, 10th and 24th), the 'Oldham Pals'. The unusual inscription read 'Death is the Gate of Life', and must have brought a little relief to those who had lost loved ones in that terrible conflict.

Looking up High Street from the Town Hall balcony just after the unveiling of the War Memorial. The crowd that day was estimated at 10,000, with another 2,000 in the parade. The Bishop of Manchester, Dr Temple, gave the blessing and 'one of the finest memorials in the north of England' took its proud place in the very centre of Oldham. One man who is not given much mention is Tom Taylor, the architect responsible for the overall positioning and elevation of the whole memorial.

It is over. The crowd in the churchyard and the dignitaries have gone, but for hours afterwards the ordinary folk of Oldham filed past the monument. Years later, Second World War victims' names were added, and today the memorial is still well looked after. The pages of the Book of Remembrance are turned, and Oldham people still have pride in their War Memorial.

Some of Oldham's soldiers outside Mumps station, *c.* 1919. Local newspapers tell us that the Oldham Territorials returned from the war on 10 April 1919; many of them had not seen the town for nearly five years. They arrived at Clegg Street station at 5.30 p.m. in real heavy drizzle, and a large crowd turned out to cheer and greet them.

The Northern Primitive Methodists (established 1865) parading down Rochdale Road, passing Mitchell Street, *c.* 1900. It looks like a large procession, but they did not go in for many decorations; with no flowers, flags and ribbons, the band was their only concession to frivolity.

Oldham Salvation Army Band, *c.* 1900. The grim expressions on their faces could reflect the fight they had against poverty, cruelty and drink at that time. They brought a little cheerfulness and music into the lives of the working classes of Oldham, and the organisation has a lot to be proud of.

Oldham Police Band, 1890. A century ago everyone loved a band and was either in one or supported one. Band contests were popular and well attended, and in 1890 Oldham boasted no fewer than six prize bands.

The 3rd Oldham Boy Scouts. This picture is a bit of a mystery, and I hope someone will be able to solve it. The gentleman sitting next to the Scout master is wearing a mortarboard and it is obvious that he is a schoolmaster, so perhaps the Scouts were attached to a school.

The writing on the back of this photograph tells us that this is a large party of Hungarian Scouts who visited Oldham just after the First World War. They paraded through the town at the start of their visit and we see them here just passing the Town Hall. The group at the front look like Scout masters rather than Scouts, and there is more than one with a row of medals. The hut behind them was used by the taxi and carriage drivers.

Sutcliffe Mill at Shaw are having a sale, and the eager sales staff are lined up for their picture, *c.* 1916. Things do not change much, do they? 'Everything Marked Down in Price', 'Our Sale is Breaking All Records', 'No Credit Given' – but can you make out the sign with 'Good Luck to Crompton's Tank for Breaking All Records'?

A classic picture of an Oldham mill girl, *c.* 1933. Oldham once boasted it had more spindles working than there were in the whole of Europe. With all the noise in the mills and factories, many of the workers became deaf or partially so. They learnt to lip-read across the noisy factory and at night in pubs and shops could hold conversations which no-one else could hear.

Grotton Lido, east of Oldham on the Oldham/Lees Road, 1938. It was a popular and well-built outdoor swimming pool. The postcard shows off this 'Temple of Alfresco Bathing De-luxe'.

Grotton Lido, 1936. This postcard looks the other way from the one above. There is obviously some special event taking place here. Beauty queens, brass band contests, sun-bathing de-luxe, and Hardcastle's Parading Bathing Beauties were among the many attractions.

The unveiling ceremony of the Robert Ashcroft statue in the Top Walk of Alexandra Park, 1903. 'Workers' Friend' says the inscription underneath, and he certainly was. When firms were coming and going through boom and bust with regularity, it was he, as Oldham Tory MP, who pushed through a bill that workers' wages must be paid first when a firm went bankrupt. They were to be paid before the banks and before the directors; the workers were to come first. This statue was paid for by the working men of Oldham who raised more than £2,000 for it.

An unusual photograph from the late '50s and one with a good story to it. I have never seen a sign with so much real 'Lanky' on it. The building on the left is 'Tha knows – Th' Umbrella Shop a' t' corner of St Domingo Street', and can you make out the large sign?

> 'Th'art ne'er go'in off bout a' umbrella an' mac fra F. Phillips's.
> A've towd thi afore!
> If it's fine it'l mebbe nobbut just fer changes.'

Ken's Café was just here on the right. Ken (Fardian), an Indian ex-Royal Navy man, was a well-known and well-liked character in Oldham.

Oldham Cycle Parade, 2 May 1903. This was obviously a grand occasion, and captured on this postcard are some of the entrants to the parade. Jennie Jones and an Australian bushman are on the left, but ET of The Nook is a mysterious one.

Oldham Boiler Works was at the top of Henshaw Street. Here, their latest production leaves for Lees & Wrigleys, Greenbank Mill, *c.* 1900.

TRANSPORT

The modern age of transport arrived in Oldham on 31 March 1842 when the Middleton Junction to Oldham (Werneth) railway station was opened by the Lancashire & Yorkshire Railway Company. The line from Middleton Junction was so steep that the trains had to be dragged up by rope. It was over five years later that the railway line to Mumps was opened on 1 November 1847. This delay shows how much work was involved in taking the railway almost underneath Oldham. There were once five railway stations around Oldham: Central, Werneth, Clegg Street, Glodwick Road and the one used for Oldham itself, Mumps. The two tunnels between Werneth and Mumps station still tell us how hard the battle was to bring the railways to Oldham.

The locomotive depot for Oldham was at Lees on the Oldham Greenfield/Saddleworth line. This photograph shows the shed (26E) in August 1953 with three engines outside in steam. These small local engines, 52338, 49536 and 49668, were 'Compounds', nicknamed 'Coffee-Pots' by boys trainspotting. Now the shed and even the lines have vanished completely.

Inside Lees MPD (Motive Power Depot), as it was officially called. 26E was the shed code for Lees and all engines allotted there had that number on a metal plate screwed to the front of their boiler, below the engine number. A Class 9 freight engine is at the far side of the shed looking ready for duty, while nearer the camera is one of the LMS tank-engines that were the work-horses of local passenger trains.

LMS tank engine No. 42444, a 2–6–4 Stanier two-cylinder built in 1935, emerges from Werneth Tunnel and into the station. At one time there was a choice of routes to Manchester and trains could go down the famous Werneth Incline at 1 in 27, the steepest railway line on British Rail, to Middleton Junction. This line, which went via Alder Root and Stock Brook, closed in 1963 and has now vanished altogether, its route being covered with industrial estates today. (Photograph copyright J.A. Peden)

A Loco Club of Great Britain Special came up the Werneth Incline just before it was lifted in the 1960s. The 'Black Eight' stopped for a photo-call and that is what we see here.

Chadderton Power Station had its own railway system and also its own steam engines, owned by the Central Electricity Authority. Here we see No. 2 and another engine in steam in May 1955. (Photograph copyright C.A. Appleton)

This is a railway accident which happened on the line to Diggle on 5 July 1923. Ghoulish as it sounds, postcards of the crash were popular and sold in large numbers.

Another railway smash that attracted a lot of attention; luckily no one was injured in this accident. You can see the engine at the bottom of the heap, and the breakdown crane trying to clear the trucks off it. A shunting engine and its wagons from Platt's factory had overrun the points and crashed into Walsh Street at Cow Hill on 22 April 1907.

An Oldham horse tram, just after it went into service on 1 November 1880. A lot of transport services in Oldham started from just outside the town centre. The Star Inn was once the terminus and passengers were expected to walk to and from here to the centre of Oldham. This saved the horse the final effort up the hill to the Market Place. The same thing happened at Mumps, which was as far as some of the northern services came into Oldham.

Oldham got its first electric tram on 19 May 1902, when the Hollinwood–Waterhead service began. This postcard shows tram No. 7 of the Middleton Electric Traction Company which ran the Oldham–Rhodes route. Note the poor driver completely open to rain and snow and whatever else the weather threw at him. The Worcestershire Furnishing Company at 211 Manchester Street are advertised on the top of the tram.

This is 1925 and the Corporation had taken over from the various tram companies. Our card shows the No. 3 route (Oldham to Middleton), and tram No. 119 about to tackle the climb up Middleton Road into town.

This beautifully illuminated tram ran the evening before the royal visit of George V and Queen Mary on 12 July 1913. What a gleaming spectacle it was, and how thrilling it must have been as it toured the streets until well past midnight.

An Oldham Corporation tram from around 1930 and looking past its best. This photograph was taken up at Waterhead at the end of the line on the No. 20 route.

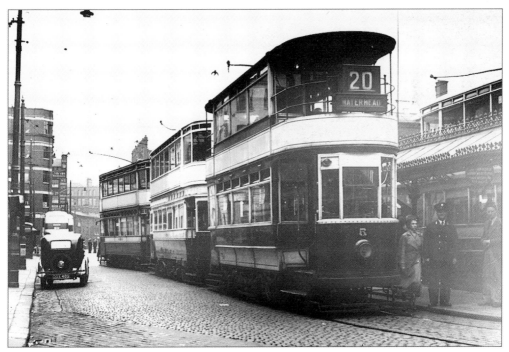

Oldham trams in their heyday. The driver stands proudly next to his Oldham Corporation tram at the main terminus. This picture, taken by the late Bill Camwell, is one of many good tram pictures that he left us. (From the Ted Gray collection)

The tram terminus at Hollinwood, 1930s. The building to the right of the far tram was the Salvation Army Citadel for Hollinwood.

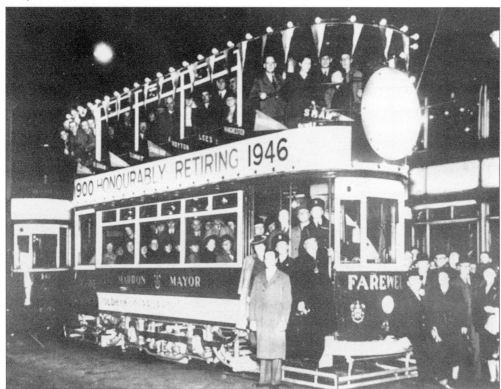

Oldham's last tram: the crew and passengers stand proudly as the occasion is photographed for posterity, Saturday 3 August 1946. That was it, the end of trams, and they thought that was progress! Now Oldham, along with many other northern towns, is looking at the successful Metrolink in Manchester and thinking how good it would be to have super-trams in Oldham.

The Oldham bus fleet, 1949. The town has always been more amenable to the bus because of the gradients of the roads and the remoteness of the outlying areas.

Oldham's fleet of road maintenance vehicles stands gleaming, and waiting patiently to take to the Oldham streets once again, 1949.

A single-deck Crossley-built bus waits outside King Street Baptist Chapel, probably 1947. The destination indicator has Rhodes Bank on it, which is on the other side of town.

A North Western Road Car Company vehicle outside the Gas Showrooms, 1951. When the North Western Road Cars (they were never called buses) first appeared in Oldham, they ran a circular route heading out via George Street and returning up Yorkshire Street.

The staff of Oldham Mumps station sometime in the Edwardian years. The station opened on 1 November 1847, when the line from Middleton Junction to Werneth was extended, but only journeys to Manchester were possible until 1856 when the Oldham to Greenfield railway line opened. Oldham to Manchester trains all ran via Moston, Middleton Junction and the 1 in 27 Werneth Incline until 17 May 1880, when the Lancashire & Yorkshire Railway Company opened a new, easier line from Thorpes Bridge Junction (near Dean Lane station) to Werneth, and this is the line used today. The line from Mumps to Rochdale opened on 12 August 1863. One line that tended to be overlooked was the Clegg Street to Guide Bridge line, which opened in August 1861; Park Bridge station was halfway down the line and Oldham Road station was at the Ashton end. It was built by the Oldham, Ashton & Guide Bridge Junction Railway (formed by the Manchester, Sheffield & Lincoln Railway and the London & North Western Railway in 1857) and ran through trains to Stockport from Oldham Central station. This service finished on 4 May 1959, and Clegg Street station along with Park Bridge and Ashton (Oldham Road) closed that day. The service Oldham to Lees, Grotton and Greenfield ceased on 2 May 1955, but the line remained for freight trains and the use of the sheds at Lee until 13 April 1964.

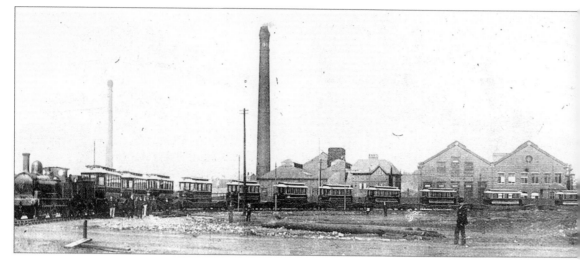

The tram cars at the Oldham Corporation Depot, 1901. I wonder what the steam engine was doing in the picture.

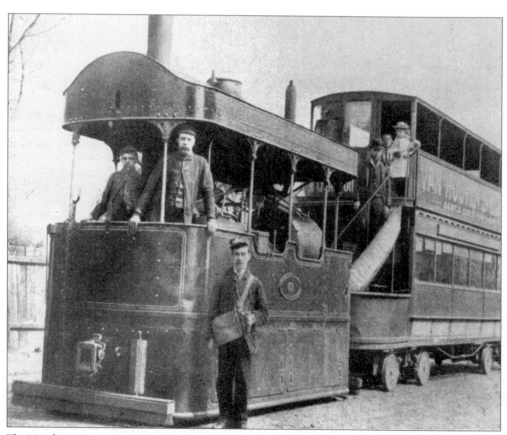

The Manchester, Bury, Rochdale & Oldham Steam Tram Company ran a service between those towns in 1889. The steam trams were basically steam tractors which pulled and pushed (powerless) tram bodies along rails set into the road. Early ones were referred to as 'street railways' and this is what they were. Here is one taking a rest at Oldham.

A 1949 then-and-now picture shows on the left the very first motor bus in Oldham, which began service on 12 May 1913, and on the right the very latest Corporation transport in 1949.

A 1946 Leyland bus (Roe bodied), one of Oldham Corporation's buses looking very neat, with no advertisements and just the town crest at ground level. This picture was taken in August 1978 while it was at the Museum of Transport in Manchester. It was last seen behind the bus depot at Oldham Mumps being renovated, so it is still in the preservation movement. (Photograph by Ted Gray)

Only the very latest and the best was good enough for Oldham in 1949, when it celebrated a hundred years of Incorporation. Pictured above was the new addition to Oldham Corporation's Road Fleet vehicles, which was the latest in road sweepers. Below we see the Leyland Limousine fire pump that was the pride and joy of the Oldham Fire Service in the 1940s.

ROUND & ABOUT OLDHAM

Oldham has grown a great deal since the original granting of a Charter of Incorporaton almost 150 years ago. Now the administrative area of Oldham extends as far east as Dove Stones and includes Greenfield, Uppermill and Diggle. To the west it includes Chadderton, Mills Hill and Royton, and to the north Crompton Fold and Denshaw. To the south, surprisingly, are Failsworth, Woodhouses and Medlock Vale. Oldham Borough also includes the areas of Sholver, Shaw, Lees, Delph and Dobcross, and many in between, including some places with lovely old-fashioned names, such as Top of Moor, Ox Hey Top, Top o' th' Meadows and Dog Hill, and the more down-to-earth Haggate, Cowlishaw and Coldhurst. To properly map out and show all the areas around Oldham would take two books this size. So here I have presented a small glimpse into the surrounding areas of Oldham, including what is, especially to the north and east, still very wild and open country.

Looking from the Golden Fleece into the Tame Valley at Denshaw. The two crosses on this picture were added by our postcard writer in 1922; the one on the right is where she lived, and the one on the left is where Mr W. worked.

GENERAL VIEW OF SHAW.

COPYRIGHT

LILYWHITE LTD.
TRIANGLE HALIFAX

A general view of Shaw, from the Sholver/Fullwood side, 1931: a fascinating picture it is too. Although you cannot see the reverse of this card it is worth mentioning; it is to a Mrs Forbester in Scarborough from Frank Whitehead of 35 Lees Street, Shaw (Lees Street is now cut in half by the new Crompton Way, the Shaw bypass). Could it be a lady he had met on holiday, to whom he promised a picture of his home town? He says it is an untouched photograph, and that there are another twelve mills to the right of the picture. The clock in the very centre of the town is above where he put the cross, almost in the centre of the card. Can you make it out?

Market Street, Shaw, when it was the main road through Shaw, north to south, *c.* 1908. The tram line was only a single line through the cobbles and setts. The shops and the street look fairly busy, and you can just make out the Pineapple Inn in the distance.

Market Street, Shaw, and almost the identical view to the one above, *c.* 1960. The shops at the top (left) have gone, to be replaced by a supermarket and Hames Bakers, but the next block is still intact. The Pineapple Inn is there in the distance again.

Milnrow Road, Shaw, *c.* 1900. I am intrigued by the disturbed cobbles and setts down the middle of the road. Are they about to lay tram lines, or were there horse trams in the area? Looking on the map of Oldham's tram system, it does not show the trams going that far up. Could it be sewer works? Lawson's Dining Rooms are on the right.

A combination card showing the chief attractions of Shaw, 1950s. Postcards were popular in the 1950s and used quite a lot for little messages, as telephones were not yet commonplace. Like other places, every village and area around Oldham had these combination cards produced for them.

Shaw's main attraction seemed to be the crossroads in the middle of the town, known sometimes by its old name Four Lane Ends. The top two pictures are from that area, one looking down Rochdale Road. The top right is marked Four Lane Ends, but it is really Market Street looking up to the crossroads. The centre picture is Holy Trinity Church and is the parish church of Shaw. I always think it is lazy when people caption the parish church without finding out its dedication. Shaw parish is in the Deanery of Tandle, which is made up of twelve parishes. Designed by Richard W. Drew, the church was built between 1869 and 1871. The bottom two pictures are of Dun Wood Park, north of Shaw, and the Town Hall and War Memorial in the West Way/High Street area.

Waterhead, *c.* 1906 . An open-topped tram has reached the end of the line at Waterhead and waits to return to Oldham. Top o' th' Meadow and High Moor can be seen in the distance. The Waterhead 'Milne' was originally just a water cornmill near Saddleworth in the seventeenth century. Later a small hamlet near Oldham was named Waterhead Mill, the original mill area becoming Old Mill Bottom. In 1682 records stated that 'the rates for the occupants of Waterhead Milne was 10 pence'. The word mill was dropped at the start of the nineteenth century – hence Waterhead.

'Bill O' Jack's Road, Greenfield' says the caption, and it shows the famous Moor Cock Inn (bottom centre of picture), alongside the A635 Holmfirth Road. Murder in Oldham was a rare occurrence and a double murder of a father and son, in 1838, with the perpetrators getting clean away, was an even bigger story. Years later, on high days and holidays, you would find people walking or taking carts out to the famous inn, and there someone would tell the events of the murder or even strolling players would act out the 'dastardly deed'.

Before television and the 'soaps' this was the entertainment of the day, and people did not seem to tire of the story. There was another famous murder in Oldham and this one was right in the town centre in 1915. A local bookseller, a Mr D.W. Bardsley, aged sixty-four, from Yorkshire Street, was found murdered in his shop on 27 July. Two Oldham youngsters, Hilton and Kelly, were arrested, found guilty and sentenced to hang. But feelings changed, and people in Oldham began to feel pity for the two young men. A meeting was held, and the Home Secretary was approached by a deposition, including the mayor and other leading dignitaries. On 15 December, the night before the hanging, there were upwards of 30,000 people gathered outside the Oldham Town Hall to hear the Home Secretary's decision: he decided that Kelly was to hang and Hilton was to serve a life sentence. This did not satisfy the crowd, and feelings boiled over. A riot started, and crowds of people marched around the streets that night; all these disturbances went on until after the hanging.

Two more views of the infamous Moor Cock Inn, where on Monday 2 April 1838 William Bradbury and his son Thomas were murdered in a dastardly way. The inn was pulled down in 1936 and all that remains of the story is their graves in Saddleworth churchyard.

Strines Dale Reservoir. The name is derived from strine (a stream). The dale where the stream flows, and the very aptly named Water Works Road, are shown. You would not think that you were only a couple of miles away from the centre of Oldham.

A view of the village of Delph, *c.* 1903. In the bottom right-hand corner is the Methodist Chapel. The name Delph comes from the Old English 'deolf', a quarry.

Hollins Road, Hollinwood, and what a quiet scene we have, *c.* 1925. This picture was taken from near Trough Gate; the Co-op on the left is still there today. The Old English word for holly is 'holegn' and Hollinwood is the wood where holly grows.

Royton, looking up Chapel Lane from High Street towards St Paul's Church, *c.* 1890. A church was first built here in 1757 and has been greatly altered over the years. The spire was added in 1878, and the church as it is today, in the middle of a pedestrianised area, was re-built from 1884 to 1889. Royton's name derives from the Old English 'ryge-ton', meaning the rye farm. The houses in this picture have now been cleared for Chapel Way Gardens.

Rochdale Road, Royton, on the southern corner of Dogford Road, which leads up towards Narrow Gate
Brow. T.H. Shepherd's, the baker's and confectioner's shop, stood on the corner.

Royton Hall, seen on a postcard from 1910. Despite the historical importance of the hall it was pulled
down in 1939 and Royton Assembly Rooms built on the site.

Shaw Hall Bank Road, at Greenfield, looking down from the station, 1951.

A delightful combination card of Greenfield, 1940. It was sent by young Les Field of Fairbanks Farm to ask the *Scout Magazine* to send him a Pen Pal form. Among the pictures are the War Memorial and the 'Pots and Pans Rock', known by some as 'Indian Head' because it looks like one from a distance.

Wharmton, the hill, from Friezland, 1963. Somewhere in those trees and over the rise is Greenfield village and its railway station. The name Wharmton is probably a corruption of Quarnden, a hill where mill stones were obtained.

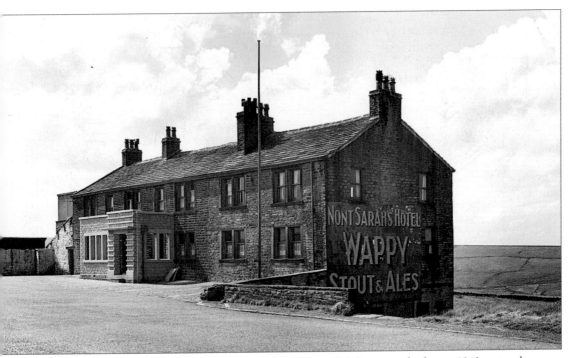

Nont Sarah's Hotel at Kirklees up the Huddersfield Road from Delph crossroads, from a 1942 postcard. This picture is probably from quite a few years earlier, because the porch that is being added is unfinished and this sort of work would not have taken place during the war. Note the impressive sign for Wappy Stout & Ales on the wall.

Dobcross, showing the steep narrow streets, *c.* 1900. This is Crib Fold and it was near here that Henry Platt (1793–1842) was born, at Bridge House. The firm Hibbert & Platt was at one time the world's largest manufacturer of textile machinery. Where the name Dobcross comes from is a little obscure, but I am told that in Middle English the local name for a malicious spirit that haunts crossroads was a 'Dob', and it was here that a cross was erected to keep them and other evil spirits away.

The Square at Dobcross, *c.* 1890. The Dobcross Co-operative Society Limited store is shown in this picture, and the shop is still there today. I like the names of the roads leading away from the cross: Platt Lane (for old Henry), Sugar Lane and Sandy Lane, Crib Lane and not to mention Nudger Green.

Knowl Farm, on Knowl Lane, south-east of Uppermill, does not look like a subject for a postcard, but this one was published by H.W. Smith of Delph. Uppermill now has a reputation as a craft and shopping centre. Along the High Street, and in the Alexandra Craft Centre, formerly a mill, there are very good shops and cafés, where you can buy jewellery, candles, paintings, and dozens of other hand-crafted goods. There is also a good second-hand bookshop on the first floor of the craft centre where you can browse to your heart's content. It is a great pity that the Huddersfield Narrow Canal was cut off by the roads in and out of Uppermill.

A picturesque view of Saddleworth, with the rolling hills and moors behind, 1950.

'Brookfield, Grains Road, and the little Knott Hill' says the caption on this 1912 postcard, published by J. Brierley of King Street, Delph, only a few hundred yards from where this photograph was taken. The row of houses was called the Industrial Terrace.

Yes, it is almost the same view as above, but looking at the other end of the Terrace. The caption on the card reads 'Barley Bridge, Brookfield, Industrial Terrace & Knott Hill'.

Ashway Gap House was the official title of this building. Built in 1777, this imposing edifice was designed to look like a Scottish highland castle. George Shaw of Upper Mill was the architect. It was the centre of the Shaw Hall Estate, and was for a time the residence of the Platt family. In 1905 it was sold for £12,000 to the Ashton, Stalybridge & Dukinfield Water Company, and was used for a time by the Reservoir Keeper and his family. In the First World War it was used as a Military Hospital, and in the Second to house Italian internees, and later POWs. The house featured in the 1970s Granada comedy 'The Last of the Baskervilles' and was pulled down shortly afterwards.

Werneth Fire Station, c. 1905. Frederick Street goes away to the right and you can see the Manchester Road façade here. The foundation stone was laid in 1897 and the station opened in 1898. When it opened, an ambulance was acquired and based at the station, the fire authorities being responsible for that vehicle. The police station is right next door.

Werneth Police Station was part of the fire station, above. The police offices were below the apex roof and the cells were on the right. The houses you can just see were firemen's and later police houses.

Coldhurst, Oldham, looking down Rochdale Road towards Royton, *c.* 1904. You can see the Coldhurst
Mill on the left, one of the many large mills that Oldham abounded in. Built in 1876 by the Coldhurst
Cotton Spinning Co. Ltd, it was extended in 1886, 1914 and again in 1922. It ceased production in 1962,
but was still used to store cotton goods up until 1967. After lying empty for a few years it was pulled
down in 1977, to make way for Boundary Park Hospital's extensions.

Maple Mill on Cardwell Street, at Havershaw, 1910. To be more precise, it is the No. 1 Maple Mill; No. 2 was added on to it in 1915. The architect was P.S. Scott, and the mill started production in 1904. In 1950 the mill was taken over by Courtaulds, who still own it.

The Delta Mill, in Crompton Street, Royton, just after its completion in 1902. It was extended in 1913 and was taken over by the Cotton & Rayon Spinners Ltd in 1950. It ceased production in 1979 but after a massive revamp, which took off the top three floors, the newly modernised building still survives today.

Failsworth centre, *c.* 1920. St John's Church is on the left: Failsworth was constituted a separate parish in 1844. The foundation stone was laid on 7 August 1845 and it was consecrated on 26 November 1846. The spire was added in 1879 at a cost of £1,843. The Royal Oak public house is next to the church, and it looks a lot brighter today with its black and white appearance. Mersey Mill chimney is next, then what appears on 90 per cent of Failsworth postcards, 'The Pole'. Here we see what was the third pole, put up in 1889 and lasting until 1924. It was 92 ft high and at its inauguration Ben Brierley, the famous poet from Failsworth, gave a speech. There is a section of this third pole and part of the fourth pole in Failsworth's new library, which now stands roughly in the centre of this picture. The fourth pole went up in 1924, and had an ornate weather cock and 'GR' at the top. This was blown down on Easter Monday in 1950, and a brick structure with a clock was erected in its place.

The first Failsworth Pole was erected as a maypole for people to dance round, and was left standing as a permanent fixture for high days and holidays. It has now evolved into the brick structure that we have today, and makes a useful landmark.

MR. BEN BRIERLEY.
Lancashire Author and Poet.
(From a Photograph.)

Ben Brierley, one of Lancashire's finest poets and writers, and a Failsworth lad through and through. It is impossible to mention Failsworth without thinking of Ben Brierley and I would not attempt to do so. 'Ab'-o'-th'-Yate' was one of the nicknames given to him from his papers, and the characters he created were all taken up with enthusiasm; they were used to name all sorts of things from cafés, boats, buses and inns. Born in 1825, he wrote his first major work, *A Day Out*, in 1855, and in it he described a ramble to a spot he called 'Daisy Nook'. His friend Charles Potter did the illustrations and based the drawings on a small hamlet called Waterhouses. Within weeks people were flocking to emulate his 'Day Out'. Waterhouses had its name changed to Daisy Nook, the houses there became tea shops, and the rest is history. Ben Brierley died in 1896, and was so admired by the public that over £400 was raised for a statue of him to be put up in Queen's Park, Harpurhey. Today, though, the statue has gone missing: it was last seen in the Lakeside Café in Heaton Park in a very poor condition. There is a blue plaque on 466 Oldham Road, Failsworth, where Ben was born on 16 June 1825.

SPORT

Work hard, play hard, is an old Lancashire trait and nowhere is it more apparent than in Oldham, where the people were nicknamed the 'rough eyds', from the otter skin hats that they liked to wear. In the '60s Oldham Rugby League was one of the hardest teams to face, and games up at Watersheddings were always a tough fixture. It is odd that the ground there, although one of the highest in the north, had a reputation of having fewer cancellations than much more sheltered grounds. Strangely, though, the very final game to be played there was due to be held in early 1997 but had to be postponed because of bad weather, and was eventually held some months later.

Oldham FC, with what was considered the ultimate trophy at the time, the Rugby League Challenge Cup, that they had just won, 1925.

Oldham Rugby League, now called the Oldham Bears, were in the past labelled the Oldham Football Team, so sometimes it is hard to work out whether the team lined up so proudly is the soccer team or the rugby team. This photograph is definitely the Rugby League Team from about 1920. I wonder if a report from the *Manchester Courier* in the 1930s had anything to do with the choice of name. The report stated that they had played hard but that their kit was ripped and in very poor condition. 'If it gets any worse', went on the report, 'they could be known as the "Oldham Bearbottoms".'

The Rugby League Team again, at the end of the 1907/8 season. Again they had a haul of silverware, including the Lancashire Cup.

Hanson (Trainer), James Hodson, Jimmy Fay, J. Shovelbottom, R. Hewitson, 'Snowy' Hamilton, ? Kelly, Mr D. Ashworth (Sec.), F. Newton, Frank Hesham, William Dodds, David Wilson, J. Swarbrick.

It is strange to note that on other photographs our Mr Shovelbottom is down as J. Shufflebothem; he only played once in the 1907/8 season. Oldham played their first game in the Football League on 7 September 1907, when they beat Stoke 3–1. The manager on the photograph is Mr David G. Ashworth, who led them until 1914 when he joined Stockport as their manager. It is still a mystery why, after clinching the 1921/2 First Division Championship with Liverpool and being well on the way to the 1923/4 title, he walked out on the champions and came back to Oldham to try to stop them dropping out of the First Division. He did not succeed, and only stayed one more season before retiring.

Oldham Athletic FC: this is the team who won the Lancashire Combination, First Division in the 1906/7 season (ahead of Liverpool Reserves, Everton Reserves, Bury Reserves and Accrington Stanley), and led Oldham to the goal they wanted, entry to the Football League.

A put-together card from the 1912/13 season. It is thought to be in honour of Oldham Athletic reaching the semi-finals of the FA Cup, a great success for the team at that time. They beat Bolton, Nottingham Forest, Manchester United and Everton to reach those semi-finals, but lost 1–0 to Aston Villa in a match held at Ewood Park, Blackburn.

The Oldham Athletic Football Club in the 1914/15 season, when they finished as runners-up to Everton in the First Division. They could and should have won it! The players met and decided to give 5 per cent of their wages to the War Effort Fund. Although the authorities decided to keep the season going, one or two of the younger players signed up and headed for away matches in the trenches of France.

POSTSCRIPT

When Oldham celebrated a hundred years of Incorporation, the Corporation produced a book of achievements and glories from that century. A hundred and fifty years of Oldham as a corporation (1848–1998) approaches fast, and I know that another publication has been commissioned to celebrate this milestone.

Here is one of my favourite pictures from that old centenary book: children playing at Westwood Park Institution, 1948.

Another photograph from that 1948 publication. This picture could stand a thousand captions, all comic, but at the time it was to show how the Alexandra Park was patrolled by friendly bobbies. I will not comment on the little lady's sartorial elegance and her unmentionables – far better left to you.

A combination card showing what Oldham was proud of in the 1950s. Blind Joe's monument is in the centre with High Street/Market Place scenes and the boating lake to finish it off. When the lake first opened the boats were named after the wives and daughters of the members of the Park Committee.

Another combination card, this time from the mid- to late 1930s. The top picture has Brown's Café and Plowright Opticians on the right of it.

A well-produced Valentine card from the late 1960s shows a changing Oldham, but still Alexandra Park in full bloom.

A Dennis postcard from 1966: it seems slightly unusual to feature the Littlemoor Flats on a combination card of Oldham. Curzon Street was not to last much longer. The picture of Alexandra Park entrance captures the special effects built for the Queen's Coronation in 1953, when the pillars at the park gates were transformed into a model of Tower Bridge in London.

Oldhamers have a very dry sense of humour, some even say a blunt sense of humour, but this would have appealed to that humour. This 1911 'Mailing Novelty' was approved by the Post Office.

Don't forget you're not in Oldham NOW!

A typical card poking fun at the rough and ready habits of the middle class of Oldham.

To wish you the good old **OLDHAM** wish
A hap'orth of taties and a penn'orth of fish

These comic cards were printed in their thousands, and as the word 'Oldham' is not in line with the words 'old' and 'wish' on either side, it is probable that other towns' names would have been printed on the same basic card.

It must be the Oldham sense of humour rubbing off on me, but I have finished the book where many Oldhamers finish their journey. Here we see not the gates of heaven, but the lych gate to the churchyard of the Independent Chapel at Delph.

Even postcards showing Hollinwood Cemetery on Roman Road were issued, sold and sent. Here is one from 1907, 'printed in Prussia'. How grand the cemetery buildings were and still are. Luckily the new M66 extension just misses the cemetery.

ACKNOWLEDGEMENTS

Robert Lees is a collector of anything to do with Oldham. He runs an antiquarian and second-hand bookshop in George Street, Oldham. When I told him I was producing this volume, he offered me his marvellous collection of postcards to choose from. I am very grateful to him for his generosity, as it means that most of the photographs in this book have not appeared in other books on Oldham that I have written.

Thanks must go to all the staff at Oldham's Local Studies Library, always helpful, informative and friendly with it. Thanks also to Mr Edward Perry, one of life's real gentlemen, a real Old'am historian, for all his patient help.

I must also thank my mate Fred Fielder, who asked me to take part in his programmes, especially during the test months of Oldham FM Radio, and The Voice of Oldham. It was only through Fred that we arranged those great evening walks around Oldham town centre. A big, big thanks to all those who turned up week after week to learn a little of the history of their town.

Thanks also to Ian May and his dad Raymond for all their help, and to Graham Fitz, Gerry and Barbara Dignan, Liam, Bob, and all the others I have worked with. I enjoyed my stints on Oldham Radio. Not bad for a Woolley-back/part-time Scouser.

BRITAIN IN OLD PHOTOGRAPHS

To order any of these titles please telephone our distributor, Littlehampton Book Services on 01903 721596
For a catalogue of these and our other titles please ring Regina Schinner on 01453 731114